George Washington Carver

by Martha E. H. Rustad

Consulting Editor: Gail Saunders-Smith, Ph.D.
Consultant: Peter Duncan Burchard, Author
Carver: A Great Soul (1998) and
Great Heart of Love: George Washington Carver (2003)

Pebble Books

an imprint of Capstone Press
Mankato, Minnesota

Pebble Books are published by Capstone Press
151 Good Counsel Drive, P.O. Box 669, Mankato, Minnesota 56002
http://www.capstone-press.com

1 2 3 4 5 6 07 06 05 04 03 02

Library of Congress Cataloging-in-Publication Data
Rustad, Martha E. H. (Martha Elizabeth Hillman), 1975–
    George Washington Carver / by Martha E. H. Rustad.
    p. cm.—(First biographies)
    Includes bibliographical references (p. 23) and index.
    ISBN 0-7368-0996-1
    1. Carver, George Washington, 1864?–1943—Juvenile literature.
2. Agriculturists—United States—Biography—Juvenile literature. 3. Afro-American
agriculturists—Biography—Juvenile literature. [1. Carver, George Washington,
1864?–1943. 2. Agriculturists. 3. African Americans—Biography.] I. Title. II. First
biographies (Mankato, Minn.)
S417.C3 R87 2002
630′ .92—dc21   2001000263

Summary: Simple text and photographs introduce the life of
George Washington Carver.

Note to Parents and Teachers

The First Biographies series supports national history standards
for units on people and culture. This book describes and illustrates
the life of George Washington Carver. The photographs support
early readers in understanding the text. This book also introduces
early readers to subject-specific vocabulary words, which are
defined in the Words to Know section. Early readers may need
assistance to read some words and to use the Table of Contents,
Words to Know, Read More, Internet Sites, and Index/Word List
sections of the book.

Table of Contents

Time Line

1864
born

George Washington Carver was born in 1864 in Missouri. He was a slave. He lived on a large farm.

painting by George of the farm where he was born

Time Line

1864
born

1875
leaves the
farm

George liked to grow plants and study them. He wanted to learn more about plants. He left the farm in 1875 to go to school.

Time Line

1864	1875	1877–1884
born	leaves the farm	attends school

Most black people did not have the chance to go to school. George went to schools in Missouri and Kansas. He studied hard.

◀ the school George went to in Minneapolis, Kansas

Time Line

1864
born

1875
leaves the
farm

1877–1884
attends
school

1896
finishes college

George finished high school in 1884. He went to college in Iowa. He studied painting, plants, and farming. George finished college in 1896.

Time Line

| 1864 born | 1875 leaves the farm | 1877–1884 attends school | 1896 finishes college; begins teaching |

George began to teach
at Tuskegee Institute
in Alabama. Tuskegee was
a school for black people.
George taught students about
plants and farming.

 George (top right) with Tuskegee teachers

13

Time Line

| 1864 | 1875 | 1877–1884 | 1896 |
| born | leaves the farm | attends school | finishes college; begins teaching |

Many farmers in the southern
United States grew cotton.
But cotton stopped growing
well in the late 1800s. The
soil was no longer fertile.
George wanted to make
the soil fertile again.

 cotton field

1896–1920
works with
farmers

Time Line

●	●	●	●
1864 born	1875 leaves the farm	1877–1884 attends school	1896 finishes college; begins teaching

George taught farmers about other crops. Farmers started growing peanuts and sweet potatoes. These crops helped make the soil fertile again.

1896–1920
works with
farmers

Time Line

1864
born

1875
leaves the
farm

1877–1884
attends
school

1896
finishes college;
begins teaching

George showed farmers how people could use peanuts and sweet potatoes. He made cheese, ink, and soap from peanuts. He made molasses, rubber, and glue from sweet potatoes.

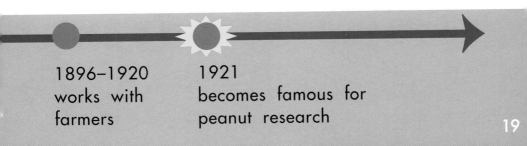

1896–1920
works with
farmers

1921
becomes famous for
peanut research

Time Line

| 1864 born | 1875 leaves the farm | 1877–1884 attends school | 1896 finishes college; begins teaching |

George Washington Carver taught at Tuskegee Institute for 47 years. He died in 1943. People remember him for helping farmers. George is famous for inventing new ways to use crops.

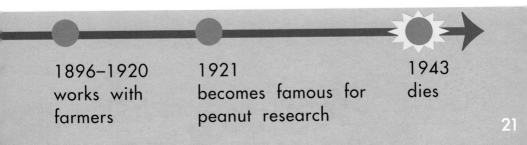

1896–1920
works with
farmers

1921
becomes famous for
peanut research

1943
dies

21

Words to Know

college—a school that students go to after high school

cotton—a plant that makes fluffy, white fibers; cotton can be used to make cloth.

crop—a plant grown in large amounts; many crops are used for food.

fertile—good for growing crops; fertile soil has many nutrients.

molasses—a thick, sweet syrup

peanut—a type of seed that grows underground; peanuts can be roasted and eaten; George Washington Carver invented more than 300 products from peanuts.

rubber—a strong, elastic substance used to make items such as tires, balls, and boots

slave—a person who is owned by another person; slaves are not free to choose their homes or jobs.

sweet potato—a thick, sweet, orange root; sweet potatoes are a type of vegetable; George Washington Carver invented more than 100 products from sweet potatoes.

Read More

Carter, Andy, and Carol Saller. *George Washington Carver.* On My Own Biography. Minneapolis: Carolrhoda Books, 2001.

Franchino, Vicky. *George Washington Carver.* Compass Point Early Biographies. Minneapolis: Compass Point Books, 2002.

Riley, John. *George Washington Carver: A Photo Biography.* Greensboro, N.C.: First Biographies, 2000.

Internet Sites

George Washington Carver
http://www.galegroup.com/freresrc/blkhstry/carvergw.htm

George Washington Carver National Monument
http://www.nps.gov/gwca

The Peanut Institute
http://www.peanut-institute.org

Index/Word List

Word Count: 224
Early-Intervention Level: 22

Credits

Heather Kindseth, cover designer and illustrator; Linda Clavel, illustrator; Kimberly Danger, photo researcher

Archive Photos, cover
George Washington Carver Exhibit, Ottawa County Historical Museum, Minneapolis, Kansas, 8
George Washington Carver National Monument, 6, 16
Iowa State University, 10, 12, 18, 20
Peter Duncan Burchard, 4
Photo Network, 14
Simpson College Archives, Indianola, Iowa, 1

Peter Duncan Burchard, a foremost authority on George Washington Carver, believes the painting on page 4 is the farm where Carver was born and grew up. This painting by Carver currently hangs in the George Washington Carver Museum on the campus of Tuskegee University, Tuskegee, Alabama.

DEMCO